BE PART OF THE TEAM!

ON THE VOLLEYBALL TEAM

STEPHANE HILLARD

PowerKiDS press
New York

Published in 2022 by The Rosen Publishing Group, Inc.
29 East 21st Street, New York, NY 10010

First Edition

Editor: Greg Roza
Book Design: Michael Flynn

Photo Credits: Cover (volleyball player), p. 13 FatCamera/E+/Getty Images; cover, pp. 4, 8, 10, 20 (volleyball) pikepicture/iStock/Getty Images; p. 5 SerrNovik/iStock/Getty Images; p. 6 https://en.wikipedia.org/wiki/William_G._Morgan#/media/File:William_G._Morgan.jpg; p. 7 Hulton Archive/Archive Photos/Getty Images; p. 9 Artur Didyk/iStock/Getty Images; p. 11 monkeybusinessimages/iStock/Getty Images; p. 15 (all) Trevor Williams/DigitalVision/Getty Images; p. 16 miodrag igjatovic/E+/Getty Images; p. 17 skynesher/E+/Getty Images; p. 19 Atsushi Tomura/Getty Images; p. 21 Win McNamee/Getty Images.

Library of Congress Cataloging-in-Publication Data

Names: Hillard, Stephane, author.
Title: On the volleyball team / Stephane Hillard.
Description: New York : PowerKids Press, 2022. | Series: Be part of the team! | Includes index.
Identifiers: LCCN 2020036960 | ISBN 9781725327795 (library binding) | ISBN 9781725327771 (paperback) | ISBN 9781725327788 (6 pack)
Subjects: LCSH: Volleyball--Juvenile literature.
Classification: LCC GV1015.34 .H55 2022 | DDC 796.325--dc23
LC record available at https://lccn.loc.gov/2020036960

Manufactured in the United States of America

Some of the images in this book illustrate individuals who are models. The depictions do not imply actual situations or events.

CPSIA Compliance Information: Batch #CSPK22. For Further Information contact Rosen Publishing, New York, New York at 1-800-237-9932.

CONTENTS

GO TEAM!

Volleyball is a game played between two teams of six teammates. It's played on a court with a net between the teams. Although it was invented in the United States, volleyball is hugely popular all over the world today.

All you really need to practice volleyball skills is a ball and a friend! You can even use a soccer ball. But volleyball is a team sport. Players on a team depend on each other. Together, volleyball teammates can make some amazing plays!

Many towns have volleyball courts. They may be at a school, in a park, or at a beach. But you don't need a volleyball court to practice your skills with your friends.

WHAT'S MINTONETTE?

In 1895, William G. Morgan, a physical education director in Holyoke, Massachusetts, invented a game he first called "mintonette." Morgan wanted to make a game that business students would play. Many business students felt basketball—another newly invented sport—was too rough.

Volleyball's popularity grew quickly among both men and women. American soldiers introduced volleyball to people in Europe during World War I. Today, there are volleyball associations, or groups, all over the world. Volleyball has been an Olympic sport since 1964.

WILLIAM G. MORGAN

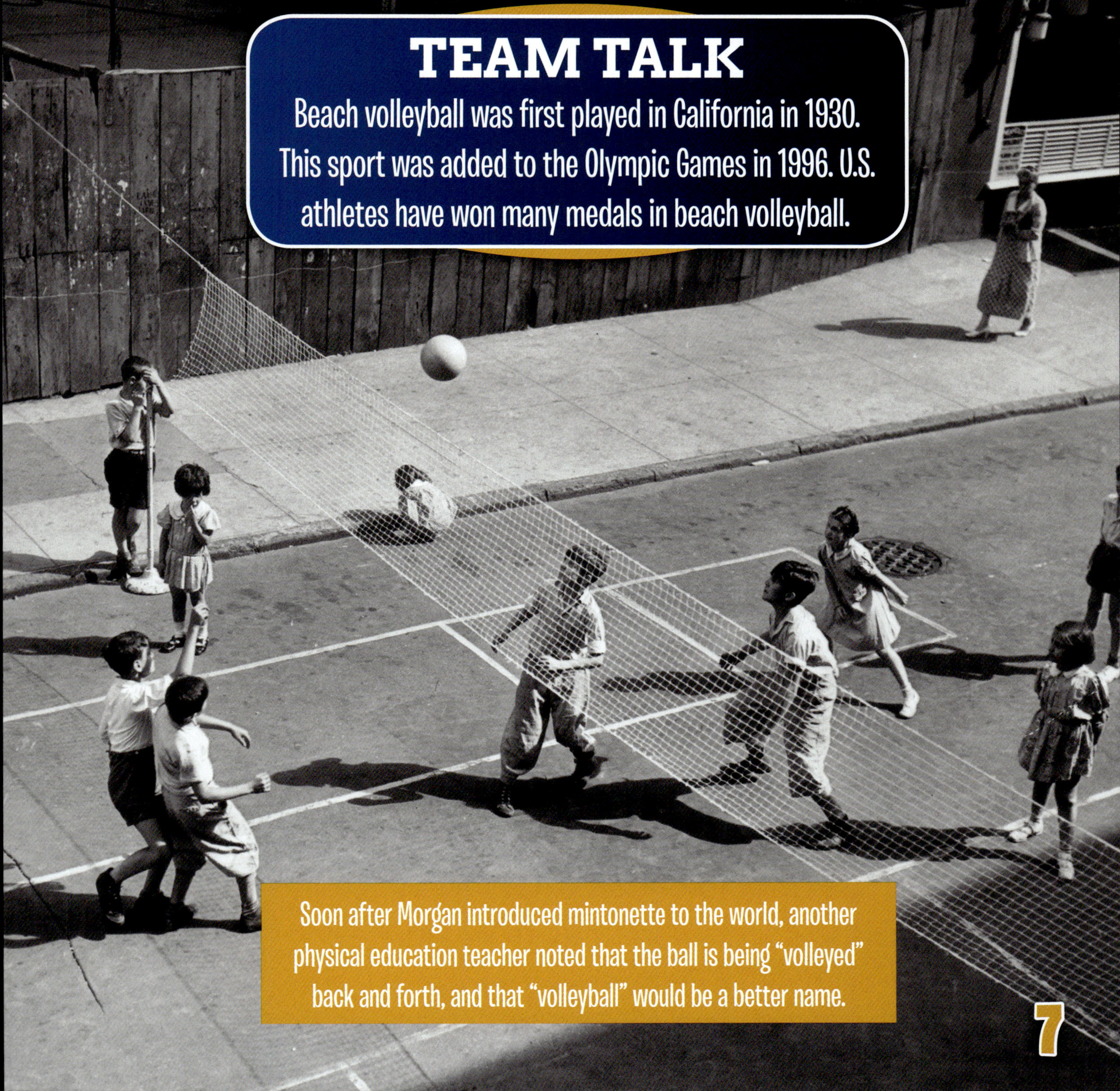

TEAM TALK

Beach volleyball was first played in California in 1930. This sport was added to the Olympic Games in 1996. U.S. athletes have won many medals in beach volleyball.

Soon after Morgan introduced mintonette to the world, another physical education teacher noted that the ball is being "volleyed" back and forth, and that "volleyball" would be a better name.

ON THE COURT

Volleyball is often played on basketball courts. This could be in a school gym or in a local park. Some communities have courts just for volleyball. People sometimes play volleyball on grass in a park or in a backyard. Beach volleyball can be played on most beaches. Some places make sand courts for people to play on.

The net divides the court in half. The height of the net depends on who is playing. Nets are usually higher for men's games.

An official volleyball court is 60 feet (18.3 m) long by 30 feet (9.1 m) wide.

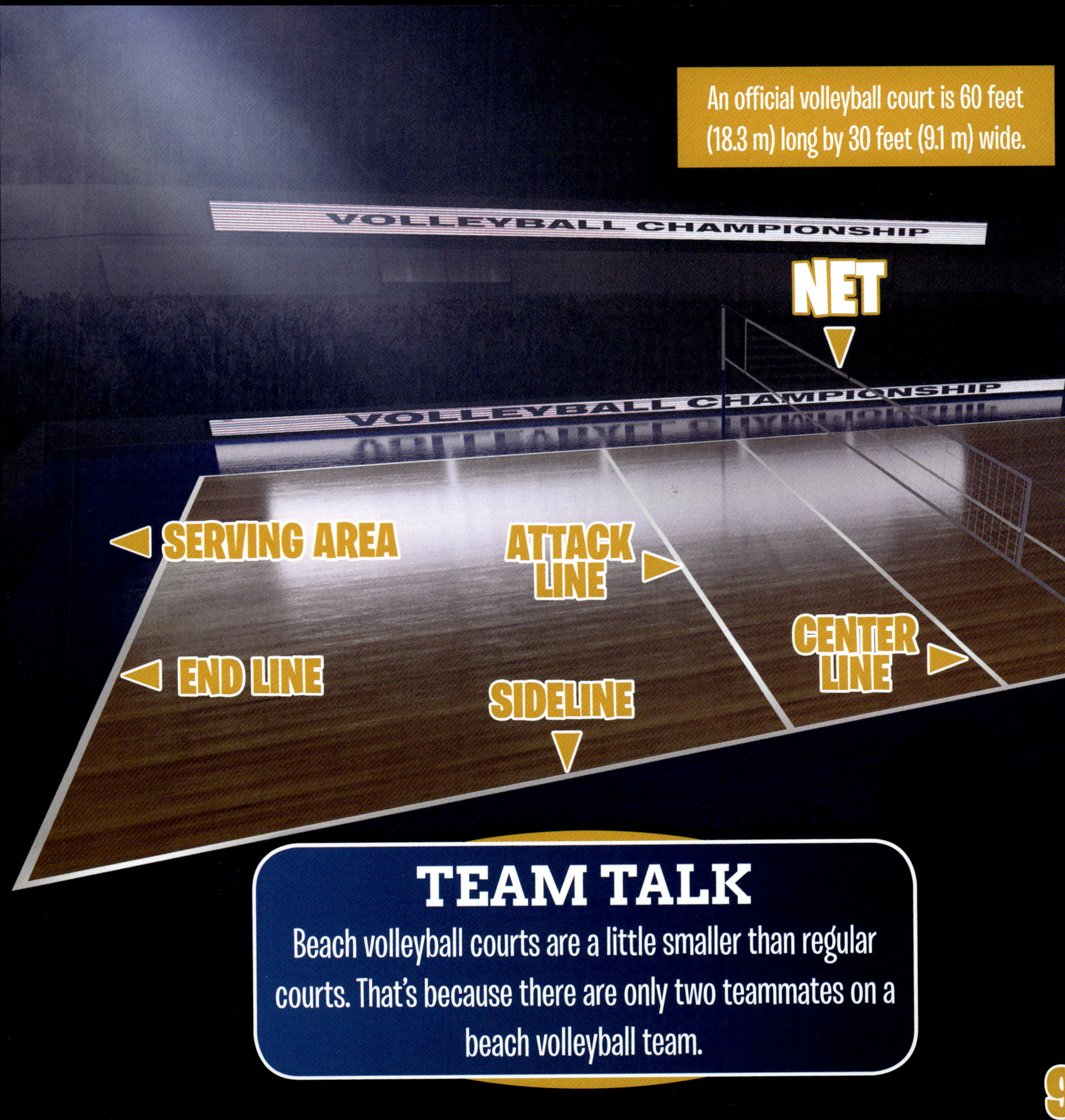

TEAM TALK

Beach volleyball courts are a little smaller than regular courts. That's because there are only two teammates on a beach volleyball team.

LINING UP TO PLAY

Players on a team form two lines. They must stay there until the ball is in play. After each play is over, the players on each team rotate. That means they move clockwise to the next starting position.

During a game of volleyball, the two teams bump and hit the ball over the net. Players aren't allowed to catch or throw the ball. A team scores a point when the other team is unable to return the ball over the net.

Volleyball games are played to 25 points, but a team must win by at least two points.

SERVING

Each play starts with a serve. This is when a player on one team hits the ball over the net to the other team. When playing volleyball at the playground with friends, players often serve the ball **underhanded**.

Good players know how to jump serve. To do this, the player throws the ball in the air in front of them. They leap into the air and hit the ball with a forward motion. This gives the ball a lot of speed!

TEAM TALK

When the server hits the ball and no one on the other team hits the ball before it hits the ground, that's called an "ace." The server scores a point all by themselves!

A serve needs to land inbounds, or inside the playing area. If the serve goes outside the playing area, the ball goes to the other team.

BUMP, SET, SPIKE!

For each serve, teams can hit the ball up to three times. A single player can't hit the ball two times in a row. Volleyball players work together to set up an **attack**.

When the ball comes over the net, the first player often uses their wrists to bump the ball to another player. The next player sets the ball. That means they use their fingers to send the ball up and toward the net. The last player jumps and tries to **spike** the ball!

TEAM TALK

Some players are thought to be natural spikers. But by practicing together, volleyball teammates learn to set up good spikers for quick attacks.

Volleyball teams don't need to touch the ball three times before it goes back over the net. Some players are good at one- and two-hit attacks.

BLOCKING AND DIGGING

Volleyball players need to be good at setting up attacks. But they also need to be good at **defense**. Blocking happens when one or more teammates leap up at the net to stop a spike.

Good servers can send the ball very quickly to an open area on the other side of the net. A "dig" is the pass of a hard-hit ball to a teammate. They are very hard to make. Players often need to dive to make successful digs.

DIG

A good block in volleyball can be as exciting as a spike and can also result in a point for your team.

RULES AND REFS

Volleyball games have a group of officials. This includes line judges and scorekeepers. Officials makes sure everyone is following the rules.

"Fouls" are actions that break the rules. When a foul is called, the ball goes to the other team to serve. Catching or throwing the ball is a foul. Hitting the ball outside the sidelines or end lines is a foul. Touching someone on the other team under the net is also a foul. Other rules refer to serving, spiking, and blocking.

TEAM TALK

Head officials often have a backup official. That person is sometimes called the second official, second referee, or down official (because they stand on the sidelines below the head official).

The official who sits in a tall chair at the net is the head official, also known as the up official or head referee. That person makes important calls about plays that occur near the net.

VOLLEYBALL VARIATIONS

Volleyball has many **variations**. In 1929, President Herbert Hoover's doctor invented Hooverball to help keep the president fit. Players catch and throw a heavy **medicine ball** over the net. Beach volleyball is popular all over the world. Some volleyball variations are played in water. Another variation is played in snow.

Sepak takraw was invented in Southeast Asia. It's very similar to volleyball, but players can't use their hands! They use their feet, knees, chest, and head to bump and spike the ball.

VOLLEYBALL TALK	
ASSIST	TO PASS OR SET THE BALL TO ANOTHER PLAYER, WHO THEN ATTACKS AND SCORES A POINT.
ATTACK LINE	THE LINE 10 FEET (3 M) FROM THE NET THAT SHOWS PLAYERS WHERE TO LINE UP BEFORE A SERVE.
BACKCOURT	THE AREA FROM THE END LINE TO THE ATTACK LINE.
DECOY	A PLAY DURING AN ATTACK WHEN A SET SEEMS TO BE GOING TO ONE SPIKER (WHO IS LEAPING INTO THE AIR), BUT IT ENDS UP GOING TO ANOTHER SPIKER.
DINK	A WEAK HIT TO FOOL BLOCKERS ABOUT WHERE THE BALL IS GOING TO LAND.
SIDE OUT	ANY PLAY THAT RESULTS IN ONE TEAM LOSING THE BALL TO THE OTHER TEAM, WHICH THEN SERVES.
STUFF	ANOTHER TERM FOR A SUCCESSFUL BLOCK.

GLOSSARY

attack: To attempt a team play that will score a point. Also, the play itself.

defense: The act of trying to stop the other team from scoring.

medicine ball: A weighted ball used for exercise.

spike: To jump at the net and hit a ball forcefully toward the ground on the other side of the net.

underhand: An action made with the hand brought forward and upward from below the waist.

variation: Something that is similar to something else but is different in some way.

FOR MORE INFORMATION

BOOKS

Bodden, Valerie. *Volleyball.* Mankato, MN: The Creative Company, 2016.

Forest, Anne. *Girls Play Volleyball.* New York, NY: Powerkids Press, 2016.

WEBSITES

Playing Volleyball
www.kidzworld.com/article/4963-playing-volleyball/
Visit this website to learn more about the history, rules, and lingo of volleyball.

Sports: Volleyball
www.ducksters.com/sports/volleyball.php
This website offers even more information about the team sport volleyball.

Publisher's note to educators and parents: Our editors have carefully reviewed these websites to ensure that they are suitable for students. Many websites change frequently, however, and we cannot guarantee that a site's future contents will continue to meet our high standards of quality and educational value. Be advised that students should be closely supervised whenever they access the Internet.

INDEX